★ It's My State! ★ ★ ★ ★ ★

IDAHO

The Gem State

Doug Sanders, Jacqueline Laks Gorman, and Ruth Bjorklund

Cavendish
Square

New York

Published in 2016 by Cavendish Square Publishing, LLC
243 5th Avenue, Suite 136, New York, NY 10016

Third Edition

Website: cavendishsq.com

This publication represents the opinions and views of the author based on his or her personal experience, knowledge, and research. The information in this book serves as a general guide only. The author and publisher have used their best efforts in preparing this book and disclaim liability rising directly or indirectly from the use and application of this book.

CPSIA Compliance Information: Batch #CW16CSQ

All websites were available and accurate when this book was sent to press.

Library of Congress Cataloging-in-Publication Data

Sanders, Doug, 1972-
Idaho / Doug Sanders, Jacqueline Laks Gorman, and Ruth Bjorklund.
pages cm. — (It's my state!)
Includes index.
ISBN 978-1-6271-3195-7 (hardcover) ISBN 978-1-6271-3197-1 (ebook)
1. Idaho—Juvenile literature. I. Gorman, Jacqueline Laks, 1955- II. Bjorklund, Ruth. III. Title.
F746.3.S26 2014
979.6—dc23
2015022185

Editorial Director: David McNamara
Editor: Fletcher Doyle
Copy Editor: Rebecca Rohan
Art Director: Jeffrey Talbot
Designer: Joseph Macri
Senior Production Manager: Jennifer Ryder-Talbot
Production Editor: Renni Johnson
Photo Research: J8 Media

Printed in the United States of America

IDAHO
CONTENTS

State Bird: Mountain Bluebird

A member of the thrush family, the mountain bluebird was adopted as the state bird in 1931. Males tend to be pale sky blue, with darker patches on their backs. Females are blue-gray with a blue tail and wings. About 6 inches (15 centimeters) long, the mountain bluebird eats mostly insects.

State Tree: Western White Pine

The western white pine, adopted as the state tree in 1935, reaches heights of 175 feet (55 meters). The trunk can grow to be 5 to 8 feet (1.5 to 2.5 m) wide. The world's largest western white pine stands near Elk River at a height of 219 feet (67 m). The largest stand of these trees in the United States grows in northern Idaho.

State Flower: Syringa

Explorer Meriwether Lewis described this plant in his journal in the early 1800s. The plant has clusters of white flowers and grows like a bush. The shrubs can grow up to 10 feet (3 m) tall. Native Americans used branches of the syringa to make bows, arrows, and cradles.

IDAHO

State Gem: Star Garnet

Star garnets are found almost only in Idaho, mainly in Benewah and Latah Counties. These stones are similar to quartz and are usually purple. The star garnet was named the state gem in 1967.

State Fossil: Hagerman Horse Fossil

The oldest known relative of the modern horse, the Hagerman horse was adopted as the state **fossil** in 1988. About thirty complete skeletons and parts of two hundred other horses have been found at Idaho's Hagerman Fossil Beds National Monument.

State Fish: Cutthroat Trout

The cutthroat trout is native to Idaho and was studied and described by explorer William Clark. It gets its name from the red-orange stripe on its lower jaw. Its back is usually gray-green, with brown and yellow sides. It sometimes has patches of pink on its belly.

The Snake River carved the deep
Hells Canyon, which runs for about
50 miles (80 kilometers).

The Gem State

Idaho, located in the northwestern United States, was once described as "a vast sea of mountains." About eighty different mountain ranges rise across the state. Many of these ranges are part of the Rocky Mountains, which slash through the center of the state, making the region one of the most rugged areas in the United States. But in Idaho, for every high there is an equally impressive low. Chains of peaks and plateaus are broken by an endless spread of lush valleys, sweeping canyons, and steep gorges.

Idaho also contains plenty of water. Sparkling waterfalls, foaming rapids, and rushing streams feed the vast wooded areas that stretch toward the sun. Idahoans prize their millions of acres of unspoiled nature.

In Their Own Words

Best of all he loved the fall
the leaves yellow on cottonwoods
leaves floating on trout streams
and above the hills
    the high blue windless skies
... Now he will be a part of them forever.
—Inscription, Ernest Hemingway memorial, Ketchum, Idaho

Sights such as the Sawtooth Range reflecting on Stanley Lake are common in Idaho.

Idaho has a total area of 83,569 square miles (216,443 square kilometers) and a land area of 82,643 square miles (214,045 sq km). It is divided into forty-four counties. Boise, the state capital, is located in Ada County.

The state is changing. Throughout Idaho, cities are growing, and many people are making a living in new and creative ways. But most residents believe the charm and special appeal of their home state will never change.

Idaho Borders

North:	Canada
South:	Nevada Utah
East:	Montana Wyoming
West:	Washington Oregon

The Panhandle

Idaho is shaped roughly like a capital letter L. The narrow northern part of the state is called the Panhandle. The Panhandle stretches toward Canada. It is a strip of land only about 45 miles (70 kilometers) wide at the Canadian border. But what the region lacks in width it makes up for in variety.

The Panhandle is at the heart of Idaho's lake country. From the shore of many of these lakes, you can spot the bright sails of boats cruising past giant cedars and jagged peaks. *National Geographic* magazine once called Lake Coeur d'Alene one of the five most beautiful lakes in the world. Lake Pend Oreille is even bigger than Lake Coeur d'Alene.

Considered "paradise" by explorers Meriwether Lewis and William Clark, who journeyed in the area in the early 1800s, the Panhandle is known for the roaring white water that rushes through the Lochsa, Clearwater, and other rivers. Boaters and rafters can pass by abandoned mines and ancient Native American rock drawings.

The area is also home to the Seven Devils mountain range. These mountains, which are part of the Rockies, stretch north to south for 40 miles (65 km) along the Oregon border. Their tallest peaks loom some 9,000 feet (2,745 m) above the Snake River. The mountaintops are often covered with snow in summer.

To the east, the dense green forests of the Bitterroot Mountains form much of the state's border with Montana. Northern Idaho is the site of the deepest river gorge in the United States: Hells Canyon. It extends for about 50 miles (80 km) and in places is almost 8,000 feet (2,450 m) deep. The canyon walls are made of black, crumbly basalt, a type of rock. Hells Canyon was carved by the Snake River, which forms the border between Idaho and Oregon. Much of Hells Canyon and the surrounding wilderness are part of the Hells Canyon National Recreation Area, which was established by the US Congress in 1975.

The rolling hills of the Palouse region, on the border with Washington, could be called the breadbasket of Idaho. Lentils, peas, and miles of wheat grow in the region's rich soils. Another of the many wonders of the Panhandle is the city of Lewiston. The city is located where the Snake and Clearwater Rivers meet and is actually a seaport. Ships travel 470 miles (755 km) from the Pacific Ocean—up the Columbia River and then the Snake River—to reach Lewiston's bustling port.

Southwestern Idaho

Just like the Panhandle, southwestern Idaho offers much variety. Farm valleys are lined with rows of corn and fields of alfalfa and mint. Known for fruit orchards and wineries, the region is also home to Boise, the state's largest city as well as its capital. Known as the

Peaceful places to fish are abundant in Idaho.

IDAHO
COUNTY MAP

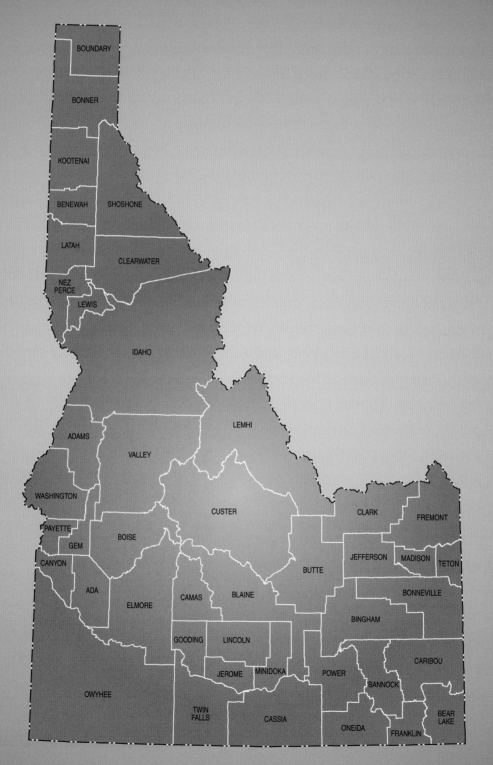

BOUNDARY

BONNER

KOOTENAI

BENEWAH

SHOSHONE

LATAH

CLEARWATER

NEZ PERCE

LEWIS

IDAHO

ADAMS

LEMHI

VALLEY

WASHINGTON

CUSTER

CLARK

FREMONT

PAYETTE

BOISE

JEFFERSON

MADISON

TETON

GEM

CANYON

BUTTE

BONNEVILLE

ADA

CAMAS

BLAINE

ELMORE

BINGHAM

GOODING

LINCOLN

CARIBOU

JEROME

MINIDOKA

POWER

BANNOCK

OWYHEE

TWIN FALLS

CASSIA

ONEIDA

FRANKLIN

BEAR LAKE

IDAHO
POPULATION BY COUNTY

County	Population	County	Population
Ada	392,365	Kootenai	138,494
Adams	3,976	Latah	37,244
Bannock	82,839	Lemhi	7,936
Bear Lake	5,986	Lewis	3,821
Benewah	9,286	Lincoln	5,208
Bingham	45,607	Madison	3,7536
Blaine	21,376	Minidoka	20,069
Boise	7,028	Nez Perce	37,536
Bonner	40,877	Oneida	4,286
Bonneville	104,234	Owyhee	11,526
Boundary	10,972	Palette	22,623
Butte	2,891	Power	7,817
Camas	1,117	Shoshone	12,765
Canyon	188,923	Teton	10,170
Caribou	6,963	Twin Falls	77,230
Cassia	22,952	Valley	9,862
Clark	982	Washington	10,198
Clearwater	8,761		
Custer	4,368		
Elmore	27,038		
Franklin	12,786		
Fremont	13,242		
Gem	16,719		
Gooding	15,464		
Idaho	16,267		
Jefferson	26,140		
Jerome	22,374		

Source: US Bureau of the Census, 2010

Hells Canyon passes along the border of Adams and Idaho Counties.

City of Trees, Boise is framed by hills and mountains. Considered a Western gem, it is the urban heart of the state.

Heading an hour away from the city in almost any direction, you enter a completely different world. The region north of Boise is "classic" Idaho terrain: clear-running streams, shimmering lakes, and steep, pine-covered slopes. This is a popular recreation area, where skiing and snowboarding are top draws in the winter. Some of Idaho's best fishing is found in the area, on Lakes Cascade and Payette.

Idaho's high-altitude desert country is to the south. It is laced with canyons made by creeks that often run dry in summer. Bruneau Dunes State Park is famous for its dunes. It contains the tallest single-structure sand dunes in North America, at 470 feet (145 m).

Central Idaho

This region is home to Sun Valley. Located on the edge of a dense wilderness, it is yet another of Idaho's recreational and scenic capitals. Here, the Sawtooth Mountain Range towers over the valley. It features Mount Borah, which at 12,662 feet (3,859 m), is the highest point in the state. The range is part of the Rocky Mountains. More than forty peaks reach heights of 10,000 feet (3,000 m) or more. Thousands of beautiful alpine lakes dot the landscape.

Central Idaho also includes the Snake River Plain. Millions of years ago, **lava** bubbled up through cracks in the Earth's surface. It hardened to form the plains along the Snake

More than half of the Snake River's 1,000-mile course (1,600 km) runs through Idaho.

River. These stretch for 20 to 40 miles (32 to 64 km). The Snake River starts in Wyoming and twists and turns its way west to Oregon through 570 miles (915 km) of Idaho. It is the state's lifeline, with some of the state's richest farmland and several of Idaho's largest cities on or near the river.

A prehistoric flood originating in what is now the Great Salt Lake in Utah sent water racing at a rate of 15 million cubic feet (425,000 cubic meters) per second north to the Snake River. The force ripped open a wide canyon. True to its name, the Snake River Canyon snakes along, dotted with boulders and sheer rock walls that drop 530 feet (160 m) in some places.

The Salmon River, which flows across central Idaho and down through the eastern part of the state, was called the River of No Return by Lewis and Clark because it is hard to navigate upstream with its rapids and swift current. The Salmon is one of the few undammed waterways in the United States. It rushes through the Frank Church–River of No Return Wilderness, one of the largest such areas in the national wilderness preservation system. The rugged mountains and fir and pine forests here are filled with wildlife.

Eastern Idaho

Geological wonders abound in eastern Idaho. The Soda Springs **Geyser**, for example, sends its column of water shooting more than 100 feet (30 m) straight up every hour. Eastern Idaho is also known for dark underground caverns. The Minnetonka Cave near Bear Lake is lined with ice crystals. It is rich with the fossils of plants and animals from prehistoric times.

Minnetonka Cave in eastern Idaho includes nine rooms of rock formations.

10 KEY SITES ★ ★ ★

Bruneau Dunes

Craters of the Moon
National Monument

Geyser Park

1. Bruneau Dunes

Bruneau Dunes State Park offers desert, prairie, and sand dunes. Visitors explore the dunes on foot or in off-road vehicles. A visitor's center displays area fossils. The state's largest public observatory is located on the grounds.

2. Craters of the Moon National Monument and Preserve

The monument was established in 1924 to preserve a 750,000-acre (250,838-hectare) "weird and scenic landscape" of **lava** rocks, cinder cones, and lava tubes. Many plants and animals have adapted to the harsh habitat. Popular activities include hiking and birding.

3. Frank Church-River of No Return Wilderness

Covering more than 2 million acres (809,371 ha), this is the second-largest protected wilderness in the forty-eight contiguous states. Mountains, canyons, and rivers abound in one of the world's most pristine environments.

4. Geyser Park

A drilling operation in Soda Springs accidently released a geyser. Workers capped the geyser and set it on a timer. Now, it erupts every hour, spewing steam up to 100 feet (30 m). It is the only controlled geyser in the world.

5. Idaho Museum of Natural History

This museum in Pocatello displays ancient fossils discovered along the Snake River plain. Included are the Columbian mammoth and the Hagerman horse (also called the American zebra), zebras, and donkeys.

6. Lake Pend Oreille

Idaho's largest lake has a shoreline of more than 140 miles (225 km). Surrounded by forests and mountains, the lake offers recreation for swimmers, boaters, fishers, paddle-boarders, and water skiers. Sandpoint is the largest city on the lake.

7. Sacagawea Interpretive, Cultural, and Educational Center

The museum in Salmon honors Sacagawea, a member of the Lemhi-Shoshone tribe, who acted as an interpreter and guide for the Lewis and Clark expedition. The center has exhibits about her life before, during, and after her work with Lewis and Clark.

8. Seven Devils and Heaven's Gate

In the Hells Canyon National Recreation Area, visitors can drive up the rugged Seven Devils mountain range to the Heaven's Gate lookout. Portions of four states are visible at once: Washington, Oregon, Montana, and Idaho.

9. Sun Valley

The snow-capped Sawtooth Mountains ring Sun Valley, and the Salmon River runs through it, attracting skiers, snowboarders, hikers, fishers, river rafters, and mountain bikers. The city offers theaters, concerts, and fine restaurants.

10. Wallace District Mining Museum

The museum contains exhibits—some inside actual mines—that illustrate the days of northern Idaho's gold rush and silver production. Tours include the now closed Sunshine Mine, which produced 365 million ounces (10,347,575 kilograms) of silver from 1904 to 2008.

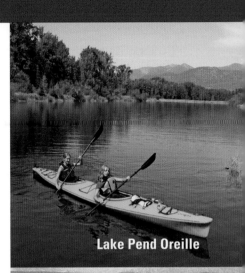

Lake Pend Oreille

Heaven's Gate

Sun Valley

North of the town of American Falls is the Great Rift National Landmark, which includes King's Bowl, a crater 150 feet (45 m) deep that was formed by a violent ancient explosion. The area also contains the Crystal Ice Cave. The temperature in the cave is a constant 31 degrees Fahrenheit (–0.5 degrees Celsius), so the lake inside the cave is always frozen.

Those who like boating, fishing, and camping are drawn to vast Bear Lake, which is partly located in Utah. The shore of this lovely turquoise lake is lined with juniper and pine. Winter frosts here signal the start of the spawning run of the Bonneville cisco, a sardine-like whitefish found nowhere else in the world.

Sections of the plains are farmed in eastern Idaho. The land is covered with a patchwork of fields where potatoes and other important crops are grown. Rolling valleys lead to the snow-capped grandeur of the Grand Tetons. This range, part of the Rocky Mountains, runs north to south along the Idaho-Wyoming border. Tall pines and quaking aspen trees make up the vast stretches of eastern Idaho's forest. There are also lakes, rivers, and waterfalls throughout the region.

Eastern Idaho has a sandy, dry landscape. The St. Anthony Sand Dunes cover an area of approximately 175 square miles (275 sq km). The dunes were built up over millions of years. Many dunes are taller than those in California's Death Valley.

Climate

Idaho's climate varies from place to place. Generally, the northern part of the state is colder, wetter, and snowier than the south. In Boise—which is located in the southwest—

Cold temperatures allow the snow to remain on the state's slopes into the spring.

the average low temperature in January is 21.6°F (−5.8°C), and the average high temperature in July is 90.2°F (32.3°C). Boise receives annual average precipitation of 12.1 inches (30.7 cm) and annual average snowfall of 21.3 inches (54.1 cm). In contrast, in Coeur d'Alene—located in the northern Panhandle—the average annual precipitation is 25.9 inches (65.8 cm), and the annual average snowfall is 52.2 inches (132.6 cm). The average low temperature in January in Coeur d'Alene is 23.3°F (−4.8°C), and the high temperature in July averages 85.4°F (29.6°C).

Idaho benefits from being fairly close to the Pacific Ocean. Moist warm winds sweep across the state from the west and help make the climate milder. In the winter, the state's wall of mountains in the east protects it from some of the cold winds coming from Canada and the Great Plains.

At higher elevations in Idaho's many mountain ranges, snow can last until June. This has helped the state earn its reputation as a skier's paradise. In addition, when the snow melts in late spring, the resulting water is used to irrigate millions of acres of land.

Plants and Animals

With such varied terrain, and so much open space, it is not surprising that Idaho is home to a wide range of plants and animals. North of the Salmon River (which is considered the dividing line between north and south Idaho), more than 80 percent of Idaho is covered in forests. By comparison, only about 30 percent of the region south of the Salmon River is wooded. Most of the state's trees are conifers, or cone-bearing evergreens. They

Mule deer are named for their large ears, which resemble those of a mule.

thrive in the moist soils of the north and include Douglas fir, Engelmann spruce, hemlock, lodgepole pine, ponderosa pine, red cedar, western larch, white fir, and white pine. **Deciduous** trees include birch, cottonwood, willow, and aspen. There are thirteen national forests in Idaho.

Hearty grasses and shrubs that can bear weather extremes are found in the drier south, but many types of shrubs and grasses grow throughout the state. Dogwood, elderberry, huckleberry, purple heather, snowberry, and thimbleberry send their roots deep into the soil. Idaho's wildflowers are often as colorful as their names. Fairy slippers, dogtooth violets, western spring-beauty, prairie stars, buttercups, and queen's cup brighten fields and mountain meadows.

The great gray owl is one of fourteen owl species found in Idaho.

Idaho's wild animals make their homes throughout the mountains and plains. Idaho has one of the largest elk herds in the nation. Large mammals are drawn to the state's rich supply of food. White-tailed deer and mule deer feed on the grasses and other plants. Bighorn sheep range in different parts of the state. To the south, bison lumber along, grazing as they go.

Stealthy cougars hunt across mountain terrain in search of a meal. Idaho has large populations of raccoon, mink, porcupine, muskrat, chipmunks, and otters. Most of these animals stay close to rivers, ponds, and streams. There are also grizzly bears, coyotes, wolves, and foxes.

River Thrills

The Middle Fork of the Salmon River is one of the top whitewater rivers in the world, with one hundred class III–IV rapids occurring in less than a 100-mile [161 km] segment of river. The Salmon River is the longest river that begins and ends in a single state.

Fishing is a popular sport in the state, and Idaho's waters are filled with many species of fish. Steelhead, kokanee salmon, and rainbow, brown, and brook trout snap at insects that land nearby. Catfish, perch, bass, and crappie are also found in the state's waterways.

The sounds of birds fill the skies over Idaho. Ring-necked pheasants gather in grassy fields and underbrush, while red-billed chukar partridges and meadowlarks flit about. Water birds, ducks, herons, cranes, and geese gather on the state's lakes and rivers.

A Lot of Water

Shoshone Falls has existed since the last Ice Age. Snake River dams have reduced water flow. But during the spring snowmelt, Shoshone Falls resembles its former intensity. The falls are 212 feet [65 m] high and 900 feet [274 m] wide. They are 45 feet [14 m] higher than Niagara Falls.

Environment

The Morley Nelson Snake River Birds of Prey National **Conservation** Area was established in 1993 to protect nesting raptors, or birds of prey. More than seven hundred pairs of raptors nest there each spring, including prairie falcons, golden eagles, northern harriers, and American kestrels. The cliffs of the Snake River Canyon provide the perfect site for these birds to nest, and the surrounding area provides small mammals, such as rabbits and squirrels, for the birds to prey upon. Yet pesticides, drought, wildfires, and decreased numbers of prey animals have affected these bird populations, and their numbers have declined. A major cause of habitat loss is an **invasive species** called cheatgrass, which overtakes the native grasses that are the main food supply for rabbits and squirrels.

Millions of acres of forests in Montana, Colorado, Washington, and Idaho have been ravaged by the Northern pine beetle. Pine beetles have turned green forests into stands of dead, copper-colored trees. In 2000, a wildfire took hold in the Bitterroot Range, fueled by the dead trees left behind by the pine beetle. Foresters are trying to stave off the onslaught by thinning forests and applying chemicals that trick the beetles into believing the trees have already been attacked.

Gray Wolf

Harebell

Huckleberry

1. Beaver

This rodent weighs up to 60 pounds (27 kg) and dwells by water. The beaver has sturdy legs, sharp teeth, and a paddle-like tail. Beavers are strong swimmers and build dams for shelter by sawing down trees with their teeth.

2. Gray Wolf

Once hunted to near extinction, gray wolves have made a comeback. Adult males weigh up to 115 pounds (52 kg) and females up to 100 pounds (45 kg). They live in packs, led by an alpha male and female, and feed on moose, beaver, deer, elk, and bison.

3. Harebell

The state flower grows 8 to 20 inches (20 to 50 cm) tall. Delicate blue and purple bell-shaped flowers appear from June to August. They are found in valleys and on open hillsides and prairies.

4. Huckleberry

Huckleberries are the state fruit. The plants are slow growers, often taking fifteen years to reach their full height. The juicy, dark-colored berries are a favorite food of bears, small mammals, birds, and humans.

5. Kokanee Salmon

Kokanee are landlocked salmon. Unlike other salmon, which mature in the ocean and return to freshwater to spawn, kokanee salmon remain in Lake Coeur d'Alene their entire lives. Feeding on tiny aquatic plants and animals, they lay their eggs along gravelly shores.

6. Moose

Moose, weighing up to 1,500 pounds (680 kg), are the biggest mammals in Idaho. Male moose have large, flat antlers and can grow up to 7 feet (2 m) tall. They are herbivores that live off trees, shrubs, and aquatic plants.

7. Mountain Goat

Mountain goats actually belong to the antelope family. They have black horns and beard-like hair on their chins. They live in high, snowy mountains and their woolly white fur keeps them warm. Mountain goats are skilled at walking on rocky cliffs.

Mountain Goat

8. Painted Turtle

This reptile is identified by a colorful shell. It lives mostly in shallow water with sandy bottoms and lays its eggs on land. It has a varied diet, and feeds on beetles, maggots, larvae, snails, insects, tadpoles, fish, and some aquatic plants.

9. Sage Grouse

The brown, tan, white, and black sage grouse lives on the plains and eats flowers, leaves, and insects. During mating season, the male prances around fanning his long tail, fluffing his chest feathers, and puffing out his orange air sacs—all while huffing loudly.

Sage Grouse

10. Western Rattlesnake

The western rattlesnake is Idaho's only dangerous venomous snake. The "rattle" at the end of its body is left behind when the snake sheds its skin. Rattlesnakes feed on small mammals, using heat to detect them and folding fangs to attack.

Western Rattlesnake

Explorers Meriwether Lewis and William
Clark entered Idaho, along with their Native
American guide Sacagawea, at Lehmi Pass.

From the Beginning

There is evidence that the first people to arrive in what is now Idaho came around 11,500 BCE. They were **nomads**, whose ancestors had walked across a land bridge that once connected Asia and Alaska. (Sea levels were lower many thousands of years ago. Because they are higher today, the land bridge no longer exists—it is under hundreds of feet of water.) The descendants of the first migrants spread south throughout the North American continent over thousands of years.

Native American Peoples of Idaho

Over the centuries, a number of Native American groups made their homes in present-day Idaho. Life was not always easy for these early inhabitants. They learned to adapt to the land. There was plenty of food in the region's forests and streams, and several groups thrived in their homes in the mountains. The Coeur d'Alene, Pend d'Oreille, Kootenai, and Kalispel people settled in the north. The Northern Paiute people lived in the southwestern corner of the present-day state as well as in the neighboring region (what is now Oregon), while the Bannock, Lemhi, and Shoshone people dealt with the tough conditions in the desert country of the south.

The Nez Perce became known for their great skill in riding a breed of spotted horse called the Appaloosa.

These groups moved about often, always in search of food. Fish was a major part of their diet, but they also hunted for birds and for small game. Women gathered seeds and nuts. In the drier regions, the women dug the bulbs of the **camas**, a plant in the lily family that was an important part of the Native American diet.

Over time, the region saw the rise of two powerful nations, the Nez Perce and the Shoshone. They were the largest groups to settle in what is now Idaho. The Nez Perce tribe lived mostly in the north-central portion of the present-day state, near the Salmon and Clearwater Rivers. The Shoshone tribe preferred the sagebrush country to the south. Horses (which had been brought to North America by Spanish explorers) were one of the reasons both groups became so strong. They gave Native Americans the ability to travel greater distances in search of food and could engage in trade. Horses also allowed them to hunt the bison (also called buffalo) that roamed the plains. The Nez Perce people were skilled riders and became well known for their swift Appaloosas, spotted horses that the Native Americans bred in the rolling hills of the Palouse region.

These two leading groups became rivals. They fought often. Parties of men clashed over the right to hunt bison or fish for salmon. Usually in the summer, though, the fighting stopped, and different tribes came together to meet and trade in peace.

Explorers and Fur Trappers

In August 1805, US Army captains Meriwether Lewis and William Clark, and several members of their expedition party, became the first US citizens to enter the land that is now Idaho. They were sent by President Thomas Jefferson to explore parts of the West that the US government had recently purchased from France, as well as to look for a water route from the eastern United States to the Pacific Ocean. Their group, called the "Corps of Discovery" included thirty-three people—soldiers, fur traders, and a young Shoshone woman named Sacagawea (also spelled Sacajawea), who acted as a guide and interpreter.

The Corps had been halted in their search for the hoped-for water route when their canoes could go no further up the Missouri River. Not far from the headwaters of the Missouri rose the Continental Divide, the imaginary line running through the Rockies that separates river flow. (East of the divide, rivers flow toward the Atlantic and Gulf of Mexico; west of the divide, they flow toward the Pacific.) On August 12, 1805, Captain Lewis and three scouts hiked over Lemhi Pass from the Missouri headwaters into what is now Idaho. Later, when the Corps reunited, it followed the Lemhi River valley north. Steep canyons of rock walls surrounded them. After several days, they met the chief of the Shoshone tribe, who coincidently was the brother of Sacagawea. Captain Clark studied the rivers in the area, hoping to take one of them westward to the Columbia River. But the chief discouraged them, and told them that the rivers were not navigable because of rapids. Finally, Lewis and Clark realized that the Northwest Passage was not going to be a reality, and they became resigned to seeking out horses to continue their expedition. The chief agreed to trade guns for horses.

Native Americans gave horses and guidance to Lewis and Clark for their trip through Idaho and into Oregon.

The Native People

The Native Americans in Idaho used horses to hunt bison and for trade.

As fur traders, explorers, miners, and settlers passed through present day Idaho, they encountered several native groups. Among them were the northern tribes living along lakes and rivers: the Nez Perce, Coeur d'Alene, Salish, Kootenai, Palouse, and Kalispel. To the south, they met the Shoshone, Bannock, and Northern Paiute people.

The northern people hunted deer, elk, and small game. They also fished, and gathered berries and roots, such as wild carrot, bitterroot, and camas. People moved in summer, following prey animals and seeking new places to harvest bulbs and berries. In winter, they lived in permanent villages. The southern people in the Snake River Plain hunted across large areas for bear, deer, sheep, and bison. They also fished for salmon in the Snake River and collected roots, seeds, and berries.

The 1860s were a fateful time for Idaho's Native Americans. The Lewis and Clark Corps of Discovery opened the door for newcomers, and few showed the native people respect. In southeastern Idaho, Fort Hall was established as a trading post along a route heavily traveled by settlers. The settlers took over the land for farms and ranches. When gold was discovered in Shoshone territory, miners poured in, taking over land and killing off the native people's food sources, in particular the bison. There were many conflicts between the Shoshone people and the newcomers. In northern Idaho, the US government signed a treaty with the Nez Perce tribe agreeing on land ownership. Yet when gold and silver were discovered on Nez Perce lands, fierce battles broke out. Miners had the support of US soldiers, and the Nez Perce, who were expert warriors, had to defend themselves. Eventually, the Nez Perce lost the disputed land.

The US government forced many Native Americans onto reservations. Today, there are four federally recognized tribes in Idaho: the Coeur d'Alene Tribe of the Coeur d'Alene Reservation, the Kootenai Tribe of Idaho, the Nez Perce Tribe of Idaho, and the Shoshone-Bannock Tribes of the Fort Hall Reservation of Idaho.

Spotlight on the Coeur d'Alene

The Coeur d'Alene people call themselves Schitsu'umsh, meaning, "the people found here." In French, "coeur d'alene" means heart of the awl (a sharp tool). Fur traders likely gave the tribe the name because they considered them sharp traders.

Distribution: Most members of the tribe live in Idaho, although some live in Washington and Montana. Many live in or near the city of Coeur d'Alene and 6,760 (2010 census) live on the Coeur d'Alene reservation.

Homes: The Coeur d'Alenes lived in permanent, small villages along lakes and rivers. They built "pit houses" made of packed earth that were partly underground. On hunting trips, they used tepees.

Clothing: Men wore buckskin breechcloths, leggings, and shirts. Women wore buckskin dresses, decorated with beads and quills. All wore leather moccasins and in winter, fur robes. Men and women both wore long hair, often braided. Women sometimes painted their faces and tattooed their arms and hands.

Food: Men hunted rabbit, beaver, deer, marmot, and squirrel, and they also ventured east to hunt bison. Fish, such as trout and white fish, were a main part of their diet, as well as ducks and birds. In the spring and fall, they caught salmon as they migrated upriver. Women gathered wild carrot, potato, onion, camas, and berries.

Tools: The Coeur d'Alene people made tools from plants, stone, wood, bone, animal hide, and sinew. Some of the items they made were sewing needles, awls, hammers, pots, and baskets. For fishing and hunting they made nets, duck decoys, fishhooks, bows and arrows, knives, and spears.

The path they faced in the Bitterroot Mountains was by far the most daunting of their expedition. Before them stretched miles of rugged, mountainous country that proved difficult to cross. The Corps was forced to head north and cross the Bitterroots at Lolo Pass. At one point, snow fell on their camp, which led Corps member Sergeant Patrick Gass to write in his diary that "they proceeded over the most terrible mountains I ever beheld."

With the help of people from the Shoshone, Salish, and Nez Perce tribes, Lewis and Clark were able to get through a September blizzard and continue west. After the Native Americans guided them out of the Bitterroots, the Corps built sturdy canoes and traveled down the Clearwater and Snake Rivers. Leaving the region, the group continued on to the Columbia River and the Pacific Ocean. They returned in 1806 and retrieved the horses they had left with the Nez Perce. They spent six weeks with the Nez Perce before continuing east to complete their journey.

The explorers proved to be the first of many. The Corps' journals, maps, and stories helped attract others to the region. Fur trappers and traders, as well as **missionaries**, made their way into what is now Idaho during the following years. Canada's North West Company sent explorer David Thompson to scout the region for furs. He settled on the shores of Lake Pend Oreille. In 1809, he built a trading post called Kullyspell House. Although it did not last long, this first successful outpost proved to non–Native Americans that it was possible to tame the wilds of the region.

The following year, the first US settlers entered the area. Andrew Henry set out from Missouri and established Fort Henry, the first US fur-trading post in the region, near present-day St. Anthony. Soon, more and more people headed for the area, attracted by the rich resources of the West. Trappers decided to test their luck in the hopes of making a small fortune, mostly in beaver pelts. In addition, British companies, such as the Hudson's Bay Company, moved in. In 1834, two more trading posts were built in the area. Fort Hall (established by merchant Nathaniel Wyeth on the Snake River) and Fort Boise (built by the Hudson's Bay Company) helped draw even more attention to the region.

Towns sprang up along the roads used by people moving west in the 1800s.

Missionaries and Settlers

In 1836, missionaries Henry and Eliza Spalding came to the area with a different plan in mind. They wanted to help establish the Christian religion on the frontier and to convert the Native Americans to Christianity. Settling at Lapwei near present-day Lewiston, they quickly set to work. It was there that Henry Spalding printed the region's first book, established its first school, developed its first **irrigation** system, and grew its first potatoes. The Spaldings were among the first white people to establish close contact with Idaho's Native Americans. Their work paved the way for other missionaries.

All this time, what would become the state of Idaho was not even called Idaho, nor was it officially a part of the United States. Great Britain and the United States shared control over the area, but in 1846, the United States was ceded the land that included all of present-day Idaho, Oregon, and Washington, as well as parts of Montana and Wyoming. The US government established these lands as the Oregon Territory in 1848. Five years later, all of the land except Oregon became the Washington Territory.

During these years, many people passed through, some staying, and all hoping to start a new life in the Pacific Northwest. Families packed their belongings and, in most cases, parted from relatives and friends back in the East, never to see them again. Wagon trains made their way along the Oregon Trail, which passed through present-day Idaho along the Snake River Plain. Few of these pioneers were tempted to stay. After enduring the blazing heat of summer and the rugged terrain, many pioneers continued to travel westward for a more favorable location.

Making a Monarch Butterfly

Fourth-grade students at Cole Elementary School in Boise pushed to make the monarch butterfly Idaho's official state insect, and their work paid off in 1992. Here is how to make your own beautiful monarch butterfly.

What You Need

Two sheets of wax paper

One black crayon and one orange crayon

Scissors

An iron

A towel

Glue

A stick that has the shape of a Y at one end

String

What To Do

- Fold one piece of wax paper in half and draw butterfly wings on one side.
- Flip the wax paper and trace the butterfly wings on the second side.
- Have an adult shave the crayons with the scissors or a knife so there are enough pieces to create patterns on the wings.
- With the wax paper on a flat, heat-resistant surface, arrange the shavings in a monarch pattern inside the wings.
- Set the iron on low heat. Place the second piece of wax paper on top of the first, cover it with a towel, and iron it until the crayon shavings melt.
- After the wax paper cools, cut out the butterfly. Then glue the stick to it so the Y looks like antenna.
- Tie the string to the stick and hang your butterfly in a sunny window so it can show off its colors!

To Mormon settlers, though, present-day Idaho and nearby Utah to the south were a rough paradise. The Mormons, members of the Church of Jesus Christ of Latter-day Saints, came to the area seeking religious freedom and an end to the criticism and violence they often faced in the East and Midwest. Staking their claims in what is now eastern Idaho in the mid-1850s, hard-working Mormon farmers cleared fields and grew crops. They helped introduce irrigation to the West, an important method for watering crops in dry areas that is still used in the state today. They also built Fort Lemhi, adding another outpost to the frontier for a time. Most early Mormon settlers did not stay, but they were followed by another group of Mormons, who arrived in 1860. Members of this group founded the town of Franklin. It was the first permanent settlement in the present-day state.

Gold Fever

With the discovery of gold at Orofino Creek near the Clearwater River in 1860, present-day Idaho was no longer a place people wished to avoid. Miners, prospectors, and businesspeople flocked to the area in the hopes of striking it rich. Soon, other discoveries followed—gold near the Salmon River in 1861 and in the Boise River basin in 1862, and both gold and silver in the Owyhee River country in 1863. The news spread quickly. Small settlements, including Lewiston, Idaho City, and Boise, soon sprang up near the prime

Seven miners take a lunch break in the Last Chance Company mine in the Coeur d'Alene region ca. 1910.

mining areas. Gold deposits in the Boise basin were vast. Miners came from around the country, creating one of the biggest gold rushes in the country. The town of Idaho City rapidly boomed and became the largest city between San Francisco, California and St. Louis, Missouri. More than $250 million worth of gold was extracted from the area. In the 1880s, silver was discovered near Wallace and Kellogg. Silver production required smelting factories, which were quickly

No Language Barrier

Eliza and Henry Spalding built a school by the Clearwater River and learned the Nez Perce language in order to teach reading and writing and preach Christianity to the Nez Perce. Their child, named Eliza, was the first non-Native American baby born in Idaho.

constructed. Railways carried the silver to markets both in the West and the East. Other mining towns popped up all over Idaho. More than ninety of these mining towns are now ghost towns, with abandoned buildings and few to no residents. The towns carry names that bring Idaho's history to life, such as Ruby City, Silver City, Garnet Town, and Bonanza.

Idaho's population was growing. Eventually, there were enough people for the area to qualify as a separate territory, and local officials asked to be recognized by the federal government. On March 4, 1863, Congress created the Idaho Territory. Lewiston was named the capital of the large area, which included much of Montana and Wyoming. Within a few years, other territories were created, and the Idaho Territory included only present-day Idaho. Boise became the territorial capital in 1864.

The coming of the railroads brought even more changes to the new territory. Mostly, it brought people, who could now move about more easily and reach once-remote places. The Utah Northern Railroad branched off into Idaho, reaching Franklin in 1874. The growth of silver and lead mines helped speed the laying of tracks in the north. By the mid-1880s, the Oregon Short Line railroad proved a valuable outlet to places farther west. Slowly, Idaho was becoming connected.

Native American Conflicts

The growing number of settlers and settlements brought conflicts with the area's Native Americans. Eventually—sometimes by treaty, other times as a result of war—many tribes lost most of their lands and were forced onto **reservations**. Although white settlers increasingly took over the ancestral lands of the Native Americans, many tribes chose to

The leaders of several Native American tribes posed for this nineteenth-century photograph.

Boise

1. Boise: 205,671

Boise, the capital, is the third-largest city in the Northwest. Historic districts tell of the fur trading days, while modern high-tech companies attract many newcomers. The "City of Trees" is surrounded by mountains and the Boise River.

2. Nampa: 81,557

Nampa has been a major railroad hub since the 1860s. It was settled by land barons who made their money from mining in nearby Silver City. There are several museums, including a Hispanic Museum, and a nearby national wildlife refuge.

3. Meridian: 75,092

Meridian was once the heart of Idaho's dairy farming industry but has since given way to suburban housing and shopping malls. It borders Boise, to the east. Locals and visitors alike enjoy the Meridian Speedway and a large water park called Roaring Springs.

4. Idaho Falls: 56,813

Idaho Falls began as a farming community, and farming is still a major part of the economy. However, its largest employer is the Idaho National Laboratory, the nuclear research facility. The waterfall near Idaho Falls was created by a dam.

5. Pocatello: 54,255

Pocatello is a major western railroad hub and the home to Idaho State University. The city has historic buildings, parks, museums, an arboretum, and a zoo. The Fort Hall Reservation of the Shoshone-Bannock tribe is nearby.

Idaho Falls

IDAHO

6. Caldwell: 46,237

Caldwell is very hot in summer, but the nearby wine grapes thrive on the climate. There are also many orchards producing cherries, plums, pears, tangerines, and apples. Caldwell is home to the College of Idaho, the state's oldest four-year college.

7. Coeur d'Alene: 44,137

Coeur d'Alene is a popular resort town located on Lake Coeur d'Alene. People flock there to enjoy swimming, boating, fishing, cycling, and hiking. The city is near ski areas, such as Schweitzer Mountain, so it attracts winter visitors as well.

8. Twin Falls: 44,125

Twin Falls is hot in summer and very dry. But in the early 1900s, a large irrigation project pulled water from the river to create farmland. Perched along the Snake River Canyon, Twin Falls offers boating, swimming, and fishing.

9. Lewiston: 31,894

Set along the Clearwater and Snake Rivers, Lewiston is a seaport. Barges from the Pacific Ocean ferry goods to and from the interior of the Northwest. Lewiston has a large lumber mill as well as packing and shipping companies.

10. Post Falls: 27,574

This rapidly growing city in the Panhandle is surrounded by mountains and the Spokane River. Frederick Post established the city and used a nearby waterfall to operate his sawmill. Today, the city offers outdoor activities from water sports to snow sports.

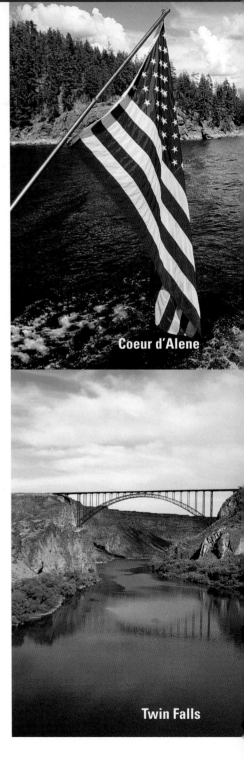

Coeur d'Alene

Twin Falls

Mine Disaster

The Sunshine Mine near Kellogg was the richest silver mine in the United States, producing more than 360 million ounces [10.2 million kilograms] of silver during its history. In 1972, the Sunshine Mine exploded, killing ninety-one miners, one of the worst mining disasters in the nation.

resist. However, the Native Americans were thoroughly outmatched and outgunned by the US Army.

The Lemhi-Shoshone people lived on land that lay along the most frequented trails to the Pacific and interacted often with settlers. The winter of 1863 was especially harsh, and the Lemhi-Shoshone people were on the verge of starvation. On January 29, US Army soldiers attacked the Lemhi-Shoshone communities and slaughtered nearly five hundred people. Called the Bear River Massacre, it was the largest death toll of Native Americans inflicted by the US Army in the country. Also in 1863, the US Army and Nez Perce leaders signed a treaty that ordered the Nez Perce people to live on reservation lands much smaller than their traditional territory. But two other Nez Perce chiefs, Chief Joseph of the Oregon Nez Perce and Chief White Bird of the Salmon River area Nez Perce, refused. When the US Army gave the chiefs a final order to remove themselves to a reservation, some of Chief White Bird's warriors killed four settlers. A battle known as the Battle of White Bird Canyon ensued in June of 1877. In a turn from the usual outcome, 34 US soldiers were killed while all Nez Perce warriors survived.

Chief Joseph of the Nez Perce wanted to avoid further fighting. He also did not want to move to a reservation. He led his people toward Canada, taking a winding course through Idaho, Montana, and Wyoming. They engaged in battles along the way with the US troops pursuing them, and although they were outnumbered, the Native Americans avoided capture for months. Finally, in October 1877, the troops caught up with the Nez Perce, and Chief Joseph was forced to surrender. When captured, Chief Joseph lamented that so many of his people had died and that children were freezing and starving to death. Chief Joseph was imprisoned until 1885 and died in 1904.

Statehood

By the late 1800s, many people in Idaho wanted their territory to become a state. In 1889, in preparation for statehood, Idaho adopted its constitution. The next year, on

People in Boise celebrated Idaho's statehood with a parade on July 4, 1890.

July 3, 1890, the territory officially became the forty-third state. At the time, the Idaho population was 88,548.

Statehood came at a time when Idaho's economy was stronger than ever. A second mining boom had begun in 1882 with the discovery of more gold in the Panhandle. But it was silver that was to prove to be the area's true treasure. Lead became an important resource as well.

Despite the success of the mining industry, tensions were rising. Miners and mine owners disagreed over wages and working conditions, and the miners organized into unions. When the miners went on strike, the owners responded by hiring nonunion workers to keep the mines in operation. This only angered the miners all the more. In 1892, the area around Coeur d'Alene became the site of an all-out war after some miners used dynamite to blow up the Frisco Mine near Wallace. The governor declared martial law. Under martial law, regular law enforcement is suspended, and the military is used to enforce the law. Federal troops were called in, and with their help, the violence ended.

Gem of a Name

The word Idaho is a made-up name. A mining promoter named George Willing suggested the name and told the US Congress that it was a Shoshone name meaning "Gem of the Mountains." Congress did not discover the fib until the name had been officially adopted.

Meanwhile, miners who were sent to jail formed a new union, the Western Federation of Miners (WFM), in 1893.

The conflict was to have far-reaching effects. Some miners never forgot the struggles of the early 1890s, and there were other violent confrontations in later years. In 1905, Frank Steunenberg, the governor from 1897 to 1901, was assassinated. He was killed by a bomb that was triggered when he opened his front gate. A member of the WFM, Harry Orchard, confessed to the crime, claiming that he had not acted alone. He stated that top union officials knew about the plot and helped plan the bombing. Their 1907 trial attracted worldwide attention. Famed lawyer Clarence Darrow defended the union officials. They were found not guilty. Orchard was

Farmers set up a sawmill with the help of a loan from the federal government during the Great Depression.

found guilty, and he was sentenced to life in prison for his role in the murder.

The struggles showed how important the mining industry was to the state. The success of mining helped boost another part of the state's economy—agriculture. Farmers needed to raise food in order to feed the large number of miners. At the end of the century, ranching also expanded. The spread of the railroads meant ranchers could send meat to a wider range of places. However, conflict arose here as well, as sheep ranchers and cattle ranchers fought over who controlled the land their livestock grazed on.

The First Half of the Twentieth Century

In the early twentieth century, agriculture became even more vital to the state. Still, it was often hard to coax a living out of the land. "I am not encouraging the countrymen to come," wrote Josef Zpevacek to his relatives in Eastern Europe in 1905, "because the country side is not pleasant at all: it is very dry, trees are in the distance of 50 miles; summer temperatures reach up to 106." The state government decided to aid its farmers. Dams, reservoirs, and irrigation projects helped open more land to farming and ensure stronger harvests. Farms and ranches grew across the state.

When the United States entered World War I (1914–1918) in 1917, Idaho was ready. High demand for food around the United States meant the nation needed as many crops as the state's fields could provide. Idaho farmers borrowed money to upgrade and modernize their farms. After the war, when the demand for food dropped, the farmers had difficulties repaying the loans. Their problems continued during the **Great Depression**, a period of severe economic hard times that began in 1929 and continued into the 1930s. People throughout Idaho and the rest of the United States suffered during the Depression. Banks failed. Many people were out of work and scrambled to find a job, any job, that would help feed their families. The federal government stepped in to help, setting up agencies to provide jobs. In 1933, President Franklin Roosevelt created an

Water cools a nuclear reactor at the
Idaho National Reactor Testing Station.

agency called the Civilian Conservation Corps (CCC), which employed more than twenty-eight thousand people in Idaho. They worked to preserve and improve the state's forests, roads, and public lands.

Slowly, things improved. Idaho's first highway opened in 1938, connecting even more of the state's remote regions. World War II (1939–1945), which the United States entered in 1941, helped put an end to the hard times. Jobs were plentiful as factories produced supplies and arms needed on the battlegrounds of Asia and Europe. Once again, Idaho's farmers were called upon to feed thousands of hungry soldiers.

Ancient Ancestor

In 1989, highway workers discovered the fossilized skeleton of a woman in a gravel quarry near Buhl, Idaho. Scientists estimate she is 10,600 years old, the oldest human skeleton yet found in North America. Considered an ancestor to the Shoshone-Bannock people, her remains were given to the tribe for burial.

During World War II, when the United States was fighting against Japan, Idaho was part of a dark chapter in the nation's history. The US government questioned the loyalty of Japanese Americans. Fearing that the Japanese Americans living in the West would help the Japanese navy attack the Pacific coast, the government wrenched Japanese Americans from their homes, farms, and businesses, and sent them to remote internment camps in the West and Southwest. There was no evidence that Japanese Americans were disloyal. Nevertheless, more than 120,000 people were forced to leave their homes, jobs, and communities and were moved into these camps. The Idaho internment camps were Camp Minidoka in southern Idaho and Camp Kooskia in the north. In 1945, the people held in the camps were freed, but many found it hard to return to their normal lives. For many, their faith in America had been taken from them.

After the war, Idaho became an energy leader, harnessing nuclear power for peaceful purposes. In December 1951, at the Idaho National Reactor Testing Station near Idaho Falls, nuclear power was used to create electricity for the first time. The nearby town of Arco became the first city in the world where electricity was generated by nuclear power

Recent Times

During the second half of the twentieth century, Idaho was influenced by many of the same shifts and trends that affected the rest of the nation. Manufacturing and other

Water Damage

On June 5, 1976, the Teton Dam collapsed along the Snake River, flooding tens of thousands of acres of farmland, killing eleven people, damaging three thousand homes, and causing more than $2 billion in damages. The dam has never been rebuilt and steep, crumbling cliffs are all that remain.

industries replaced farming as the main source of income. Cities and their suburbs grew as people moved from rural areas.

Today, the nuclear facilities near Idaho Falls are known as the Idaho National Laboratory (INL). The INL is a research facility that researches nuclear power and safety, alternative energy, nuclear waste management, and cybersecurity. It has built fifty-two nuclear reactors on the site, but currently operates only three.

By the end of the twentieth century and into the twenty-first, the United States again fell into economic hard times. Idaho's mining and logging industries saw a decline. However, as the nation's economy recovered, not only did the natural resource-based industries improve, but new high-technology businesses cropped up in some of the state's urban centers. Numerous outdoor recreation activities attracted more and more tourists. Meanwhile, Idaho's population grew as more people were drawn to new opportunities and the state's natural beauty. The state's population increased by almost 30 percent in the 1990s and by more than 20 percent between 2000 and 2010. Population estimates for the next decade continue to rise.

As Idaho moves forward in the twenty-first century, citizens will be frequently expected to make choices and compromises between jobs and economic growth and environmental conservation.

10 KEY DATES IN STATE HISTORY

1. **11,500 BCE**

First people, ancestors of Bannock, Coeur d'Alene, Kootenai, Kalispel, Nez Perce, Paiute, Pend d'Oreille, and Shoshone people, first made their homes in Idaho.

2. **August 12, 1805**

Captain Meriwether Lewis and three scouts cross the Continental Divide into Idaho at Lemhi Pass.

3. **1860**

Gold is first discovered at Orofino Creek. Franklin, the state's first permanent town built by people of European descent, is established.

4. **March 4, 1863**

The Idaho Territory is created, and Boise is named its capital. Boise replaced Lewiston as the capital because it was easier to reach. Montana broke away from the territory in 1864, and Wyoming left in 1868.

5. **July 3, 1890**

Idaho becomes the forty-third state. The state's new constitution placed the University of Idaho in Moscow.

6. **December 20, 1951**

Near Idaho Falls, electricity is produced for the first time using nuclear energy.

7. **June 1975**

The Columbia-Snake Inland River Waterway is finished with the completion of the Lower Granite Dam, making Lewiston the farthest-inland seaport in the West. Construction of a series of dams and locks had started in the 1930s.

8. **February 1, 1997**

Linda Copple Trout, the first woman to be appointed to Idaho's Supreme Court, is elected Chief Justice of the Idaho Supreme Court.

9. **May 5, 2011**

Idaho resumes management of gray wolves in the state after the animals are removed from the federal endangered species list.

10. **May 26, 2014**

The sole US prisoner of war in Afghanistan, Idaho resident Bowe Bergdahl, was released by his Taliban captors in an exchange of prisoners.

The student cheering section at a
Boise State University basketball
game reflects the population of Idaho.

The People

In 2000, a problem arose at the University of Idaho. A graphic artist working for the school was asked to create an advertisement to recruit new students. He looked in the school's files and could not find any photographs that showed students of races other than white. So he used computer software to change a photograph of a group of white students so that it appeared some of them were African American or Asian American. When the news leaked, people were upset. The president of the university explained that they did not want to offend anyone but simply wanted to express a commitment to promoting a diverse student population. But the student population did in fact reflect the overall white majority in the state. According to the 2010 US Census, 89.1 percent of Idaho's population is white. Nonetheless, many people of other races and ethnicities have played major roles in shaping the character of the state throughout its history.

Idaho's population has undergone many changes in the last few centuries. In the days of Lewis and Clark, English was not yet spoken in Idaho. The Corps met Native Americans who spoke Spanish as well as native languages. During the fur-trading days, French Canadians introduced the French language to the region. They left their mark on Idaho place names, such as Boise, which means "wooded," and Pend Oreille, meaning "earring," which they thought the lake resembled. Also during the fur trade, the Hudson's

Bay Company shipped furs via Hawaii, and many Hawaiians joined the company. From 1834 to 1844, Hawaiian fur trappers and traders ran Fort Boise. The name Owyhee, given to a mountain range, a county, and a river, honors the Hawaiians. Owyhee is an early spelling of "Hawaii."

The mining boom attracted people from Mexico, Europe, and China, as well as US citizens of African and European descent. Today, most Idahoans are descendants of settlers of English, Irish, and Scottish origin who came to the area from the East and the Midwest. Descendants of people of French, Swiss, German, Czech, Polish, Slovak, and Scandinavian origin also add to the state's ethnic mix.

Hispanics

Today, as in many other US states, Hispanic Americans make up the fastest-growing population group in Idaho. In 2010, Hispanics (people who trace their origins to a Spanish-speaking culture) made up more than 11 percent of Idaho's population. According to the US Bureau of the Census, the number of Hispanic people in Idaho increased by 73 percent between 2000 and 2010.

Most of the Hispanic people in Idaho are of Mexican descent, but others trace their origins to many parts of the Spanish-speaking world. People of Central American heritage, especially Guatemalan and Honduran backgrounds, are settling in the Treasure Valley area of southwestern Idaho. The state has even been called a Hispanic melting pot.

Hispanic Americans are Idaho's fastest growing cultural group.

Some Hispanic Americans have been living in Idaho for generations, and others have recently arrived.

The Hispanic women's organization Mujeres Unidas de Idaho (United Women of Idaho) was once mostly made up of Mexican Americans. Over the years, it has grown to include many members from other Hispanic backgrounds. Among its activities, Mujeres Unidas works to encourage Hispanic-American women to take leadership roles in their communities. Various organizations in Idaho strive to preserve Hispanic traditions and address issues that affect the Hispanic community. They support programs to improve education and health care for Hispanic communities. Moreover, many of the newcomers arrive with limited knowledge of English. Consequently, businesses and government agencies are hiring more bilingual employees or offering their workers Spanish-language classes.

Basques

Beginning in the late 1800s, and especially between 1900 and 1920, a large number of Basque immigrants came to Idaho from the Pyrenees Mountains region of Spain and France. They worked mostly as sheepherders and ranchers. The Basque people settled in Europe before other European groups, and at times there has been political conflict between the Basques and their neighbors. So, too, there have been waves of Basque emigration, and in the nineteenth century, many left Europe for North and South

Children of Basque heritage wear traditional clothing during a dance at Boise's annual festival in honor of St. Ignatius of Loyola. St. Ignatius was from a Basque family.

★ 10 ★ KEY PEOPLE ★ ★

Ezra Taft Benson

Bill Fagerbakke

Harmon Killebrew

1. Ezra Taft Benson

Ezra Taft Benson was born in Whitney to a Mormon farm family. He started an Idaho farmer's cooperative. In 1953, President Eisenhower appointed him Secretary of Agriculture. He later became president of the Church of Jesus Christ of Latter-day Saints.

2. Carol Ryrie Brink

Children's author Carol Ryrie Brink was born in 1895 in Moscow and was raised by her grandmother. She attended the University of Idaho. In 1936, she won the Newbery Medal for *Caddie Woodlawn*, a novel based on her grandmother's pioneer childhood.

3. Bill Fagerbakke

Bill Fagerbakke moved to Rupert as a teenager. The University of Idaho graduate became an actor. He co-starred in a TV series called *Coach*, had a recurring role on the series *How I Met Your Mother*, and provides the voice of Patrick Star on *SpongeBob SquarePants*.

4. Ernest Hemingway

Ernest Hemingway moved to Ketchum in the late 1950s. The author of *A Farewell to Arms*, *For Whom the Bell Tolls*, and *The Old Man and the Sea* received a Nobel Prize for literature.

5. Harmon Killebrew

Harmon Killebrew was born in Payette in 1936 and signed by the Washington Senators at seventeen. He hit 573 home runs for the Senators, Minnesota Twins, and Kansas City Royals. He was inducted into the Baseball Hall of Fame in 1984.

6. Demi Moore

Demi Moore is a film actress and producer. She moved from California to Hailey to raise her three daughters. In addition to starring in several films, she also produced the three *Austin Powers* movies.

7. Barbara Morgan

Barbara Morgan taught reading and math in McCall from 1975 to 1998. In 2007, she was a crew member on an eleven-day NASA mission aboard the *Endeavor* spacecraft. She is the first "teacher in space" to complete a mission.

8. Sacagawea

Sacagawea, born in 1788, was a member of the Lemhi-Shoshone tribe. Kidnapped as a child, she escaped and married a French fur trader. The couple and their baby joined Lewis and Clark's expedition into the American West, where she acted as an interpreter and guide.

9. John Richard Simplot

J. R. Simplot's family homesteaded in Magic Valley. A potato farmer, in 1967 he made a deal with McDonald's to supply them with frozen French fries. When he died at age ninety-nine, he was the world's oldest billionaire.

10. Picabo Street

Picabo Street was born in Triumph in 1971. Named after the nearby town of Picabo, she spent her youth skiing in Sun Valley. She won silver (1994) and gold (1998) Olympic medals and was the first US skier to win a World Cup season title.

Barbara Morgan

Sacagawea

Picabo Street

Who Idahoans Are

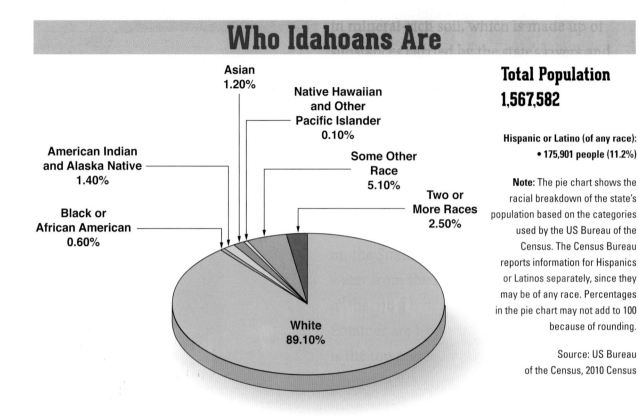

Asian
1.20%

Native Hawaiian and Other Pacific Islander
0.10%

American Indian and Alaska Native
1.40%

Black or African American
0.60%

Some Other Race
5.10%

Two or More Races
2.50%

White
89.10%

Total Population
1,567,582

Hispanic or Latino (of any race):
• 175,901 people (11.2%)

Note: The pie chart shows the racial breakdown of the state's population based on the categories used by the US Bureau of the Census. The Census Bureau reports information for Hispanics or Latinos separately, since they may be of any race. Percentages in the pie chart may not add to 100 because of rounding.

Source: US Bureau of the Census, 2010 Census

America. Idaho's rugged country appealed to them and Basque immigrants have thrived in the state. Today, Boise has the largest Basque community in the United States. It also plays a large role in preserving the Basque culture. The city is home to the Basque Museum and Cultural Center, where records, artifacts, photographs, and oral histories are available to the public.

Native Americans

Approximately twenty-one thousand Native Americans live in Idaho today. They live in communities across the state, including Idaho's four reservations. The state's Native Americans are citizens of Idaho, but they are also citizens of their own tribal governments. Native Americans in Idaho today include people from many tribes, such as the Nez Perce, Kootenai, Shoshone, Bannock, Coeur d'Alene, and Northern Paiute.

In eastern Idaho, just north of Pocatello, is the 521,500-acre (211,000 ha) Fort Hall Reservation of the Shoshone and Bannock people. The reservation is just a small part of the land that the Shoshone-Bannock people had inhabited for thousands of years. The Coeur d'Alene Reservation is located in the Panhandle. It is 598,500 acres (242,200 ha). The Duck Valley Reservation, which covers 288,000 acres (116,550 ha), is the home of the Shoshone and Paiute. This reservation straddles the state line between Idaho and Nevada. The Nez

Perce Reservation, in western Idaho near Lewiston, covers 770,000 acres (311,600 ha).

Once, many people living on the reservations struggled to make ends meet. The reservations were often located far from developed areas, so residents had trouble finding jobs. But the tribal leaders have found a way around these challenges. They have created their own jobs and an even greater sense of independence. Income from agriculture, tourism, casinos, and the sale of native crafts helps provide the Native Americans with a better quality of life.

Historians have called the Native Americans "the first environmentalists." That is certainly true of the Shoshone-Bannock people, who entrust their faith in the land that has sustained them throughout time. In defense of their beliefs, in recent years Shoshone environmental activists have spoken out about some of the abuses they see occurring around them. They have successfully challenged plans to build a high-level nuclear waste dump near what some politicians have called their "barren" homelands. They opposed the building of a dam that would threaten a site where healing rituals have taken place for generations. In 2010, they filed a lawsuit against some federal agencies to block a land deal with a private company because they said it could lead to air pollution. By working together, Native Americans have helped preserve the land they value.

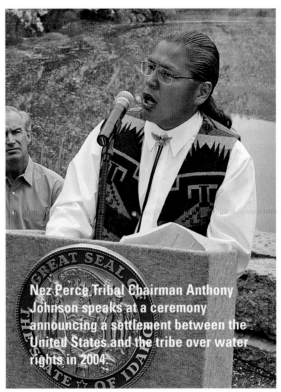

Nez Perce Tribal Chairman Anthony Johnson speaks at a ceremony announcing a settlement between the United States and the tribe over water rights in 2004.

In Their Own Words

"These poor souls were cheated in every way possible ... I would willingly give my life to help these Indians."
–Father Pierre de Smet, Jesuit missionary and teacher, Coeur d'Alene Reservation

African Americans

The first African American to enter Idaho was an enslaved man named York, who belonged to Captain Clark. The Nez Perce people were curious about his color and impressed with his skilled craftsmanship abilities. During the gold rush, some African Americans came to Idaho, most working in service jobs, not mining. After the Civil War, nearly one-fourth of the cowboys who herded horses and cattle in the West were African Americans, some of whom settled in Idaho. The Idaho Black History Museum in Boise occupies one of the first buildings in Idaho constructed by an African American.

Asian Americans

Few Asian Americans—only about nineteen thousand—live in present-day Idaho. But during the gold rush days, a steady migration of Chinese laborers appeared in the state. Mostly men, they worked as miners or provided services to the industry by running restaurants and stores. By 1870, the Idaho Territory had four thousand Chinese residents, about 29 percent of its total population. Later, Japanese immigrants arrived. Many Asian laborers found work on the railroads. Others farmed the fertile valleys. Lewiston had a strong Chinese presence and today, a museum at Lewiston's Lewis-Clark State College honors their heritage.

Many people, especially Japanese Americans, visit Idaho to honor those imprisoned during World War II at Camp Minidoka. The camp is now a memorial and testament to people who survived hardship with grace and kept their society strong and their family values and work ethic intact. People today can walk inside the barbed wire enclosures and see the bleak housing barracks and other buildings, standing alongside flower and vegetable gardens that were carefully tended by Japanese-American prisoners.

Education

Idaho's first schools began teaching students years before statehood. Missionaries Henry and Eliza Spalding established the first school in Idaho, to educate Native American children, in 1837. In 1860, Mormons in Franklin established the first school to educate white children. Three years later, when the Idaho Territory was created, the first legislative assembly took steps to make sure that children in the region received an education. Legislators set up the position of territorial superintendent of public

Micki Kawakami speaks to fellow Japanese Americans held at the Minidoka internment camp at a gathering in the office of Gov. Butch Otter in 2007.

instruction. Then, in 1864, legislators adopted a school code that laid the basis for Idaho's public school system. By the end of 1865, Idaho had twelve schools educating 427 white children. The US government gave grants to develop mission schools for native children. One mission school was on the Coeur d'Alene reservation. It was established by the Jesuit priest Father Pierre de Smet, who traveled throughout the West reaching out with sympathy toward the Native Americans.

In the early years of Idaho as a territory and a state, education was not free and equal. From 1866 to 1871, all non-white children were banned from attending public school. By 1873, race was no longer in the law books, and in 1899, a young black woman named Jenny Hughes was the first African American to graduate from the University of Idaho. Native Americans also had a difficult time receiving a fair education. The thinking at the time was that the best way to educate Native American children was to force them to adopt white culture and erase their native culture. Many native children not attending mission schools were taken from their families and sent to strict "Indian boarding schools," some as far away as Pennsylvania. The schools cut the children's hair, dressed them in "white man's clothing," and forced them to speak, write, and read only in English. These schools continued into the early 1920s.

Today, education is among the many state issues that are important to Idaho citizens, no matter what their race or background. They know that while some of their schools are successful, others face hard times and new challenges. During the first decade of the twenty-first century, a time of economic difficulty in Idaho and the rest of the United States, the state budget for Idaho schools was cut. This meant that students attended school for fewer days, went on fewer field trips, and had fewer chances to take classes in such areas as music and art. To this day, lawmakers and citizens are trying to agree on how to manage school budgets and reform.

Idaho has three state universities. The University of Idaho, located in Moscow, is the oldest. It was founded by the territorial legislature in 1889. The university has more than twelve thousand students and the only law school in Idaho. Boise State University, founded in Boise in 1932, is the largest university, with about 19,660 students in 2014. Idaho State University, in Pocatello, was founded in 1901 and has about 14,500 students in 2014.

Lewis-Clark State College, in Lewiston, is a four-year state college. In addition, Idaho has four two-year state colleges. There are also a number of private colleges and universities in the state, including Ricks College in Rexburg, the largest private two-year college in the nation.

Lionel Hampton Jazz Festival

McCall Winter Carnival

1. Cherry Festival

The Payette River town of Emmett celebrates its cherry harvest in June. Emmett charms festivalgoers with pie-eating and cherry pit–spitting contests, a pie bake-off, a parade, a carnival, a quilt show, concerts, and square dancing.

2. Lionel Hampton Jazz Festival

Some of the world's leading jazz musicians perform as well as offer workshops for students of all ages at this four-day event held at the University of Idaho each February.

3. McCall Winter Carnival

An ice sculpture contest is the highlight of this festival held on the frozen shores of Lake Payette in late January and early February. To celebrate Mardi Gras, this ten-day party features fireworks, parades, snowshoe golf, tubing, and snowbike races.

4. Murphy's Outpost Days

In early summer, Murphy celebrates its frontier past with longhorn cattle drives, cowboy poetry, and "lost art" demonstrations of silversmithing, quilting, basket making, and gold panning. There's an art show, a fast-draw contest, and a Horned Toad Race.

5. Priest Lake Sled Dog Races

February brings the Pacific Northwest Champion Sled Dog races to Nordman. Fans at the finish line cheer mushers and their highly trained huskies, malamutes, Samoyeds, and more. There are also races for mushers ages 8-14.

6. Shoshone-Bannock Festival

In August, the Shoshone-Bannock tribes host a powwow at their Fort Hall Reservation, featuring a rodeo, golf and softball tournaments, foot races, traditional handgame tournaments, and indigenous children's games. The entertainment also includes dancing, traditional foods, music, chants, and drumming.

7. Snake River Stampede

This top-rated rodeo kicks off every July in Nampa. Events include bronco riding, calf roping, steer wrestling, and barrel racing. Visitors can enjoy a "Buck-a-roo breakfast" a parade, and the famous Snake River Stampeders Night Light Drill Team.

8. Spud Day

Shelley celebrates Idaho's "Famous Potatoes" in September. Events include a "spud tug," a potato-picking contest, and a demolition derby. The Spud Day parade features an airplane that drops ping-pong balls on spectators.

9. The Trailing of the Sheep Festival

Wood River Valley residents celebrate their sheep-raising heritage in October with three days of food, crafts, music, and dancing performed by the groups that settled the area— Basque, Scottish, Polish and Peruvian. At festival's end, sheep are herded from the mountains onto Main Street.

10. Western Idaho Fair

Idaho's oldest and largest fair runs for ten days in August in Boise. The fair, which started in 1897, spotlights the state's history and people. There are concerts, carnival rides, exhibits, crafts booths, kids' programs, and animal shows.

Shoshone-Bannock Festival

Western Idaho Fair

Light floods into the state capitol building through windows in the beautiful dome.

How the Government Works

In 2014, the Idaho legislature established March 4 as "Idaho Day," to commemorate the creation of the Idaho Territory in 1863. Residents of the territory were eager and ready to have more control over the way their government worked.

Today, three major levels of government serve the needs of the citizens of Idaho: federal, state, and local. Idaho sends two senators and, as of 2015, two members to the US House of Representatives. (A state's population determines the number of house representatives that go to Washington, DC.) The state government is responsible for passing laws, delivering justice, and managing affairs of the state. Local governments provide services for people that are specific to their communities.

County and Other Local Governments

On the local level, Idaho's forty-four counties are each divided into three districts. The voters in each district elect a commissioner. Two commissioners are elected to two-year terms, and one serves for four years. Voters in each county also elect other county officials, including a clerk, prosecuting attorney, treasurer, and sheriff. They each serve four-year terms.

Most of Idaho's cities have a mayor-council system of government. In such a system, the voters elect a mayor, who is responsible for preparing the budget and appointing

The city of Boise is run from City Hall.

heads of departments, such as police and fire. Voters also elect members of the city council, who must approve the budget and make the city's laws. Some of Idaho's cities—including Lewiston, McCall, and Twin Falls—have a council-manager system, in which voters elect members of the city council. Council members are responsible for making city policies, passing laws, and hiring a city manager to supervise government operations.

State Government

Since 1864, Boise has been Idaho's capital city. Government offices and the state capitol building are located downtown. Idaho's legislature meets in the capitol building, which also houses the governor's offices.

The governor's official residence is a grand structure located on a hill above Boise. It serves as a center for state ceremonies, as well as the governor's social and political activities. The governor's residence was a donation to the state made in 2009 by J. R. and Esther Simplot. J. R. Simplot was the state's wealthiest businessman.

Idaho's state government has three branches: the executive, legislative, and judicial branches. Idaho's constitution was adopted in 1889 and went into effect in 1890, when Idaho was granted statehood. The constitution describes the functions and powers of each branch of state government. Since 1890, it has been amended (changed) more than one hundred times. The Idaho legislature may propose amendments to the state constitution. A convention called by the legislature may also propose amendments that must be approved or rejected by the voters.

Individuals in Idaho have the right to suggest or reject laws, independent of the legislature's lawmaking. Under the state constitution, citizens have the power of "**initiative** and **referendum**." In an initiative, voters can suggest a new law. If enough people agree with the proposal, the initiative is placed on the ballot, and if approved by voters, it becomes the law. In a similar fashion, in a referendum, voters can ask for a repeal of an existing law. If enough voters agree, the law is removed.

Branches of Government
Executive

The governor of Idaho serves as the head of the executive branch. The governor is elected to a four-year term, and laws do not restrict how many times he or she may be elected. The governor is responsible for appointing the heads of many agencies, proposing the state budget, and approving or rejecting proposed laws. Other elected positions in the executive branch positions are the lieutenant governor, secretary of state, state treasurer, state controller, attorney general, and superintendent of public instruction. All are elected to four-year terms. To make sure the state's business runs smoothly, the governor appoints heads of different departments and members of official boards and commissions.

Legislative

The Idaho legislature makes up the legislative, or lawmaking, branch. Idaho's legislature is made up of two chambers, or parts, the state senate and the state house of representatives. There are thirty-five senators and seventy representatives. All are elected to two-year terms, with no limit to how many terms can be served. Legislators serve on various committees that examine many of the important matters affecting people of the state, from education to the environment to agriculture.

The Governor's Mansion, built in 2009, was donated by J.R. and Esther Simplot.

Judicial

The judicial branch enforces and interprets laws. The Idaho Supreme Court is the highest court in the state. It has a chief justice and four associate justices who are elected by Idaho's voters to six-year terms. The state Supreme Court oversees the entire judicial branch, establishing rules and policies. The second-highest court in the state is the Idaho Court of Appeals, which is made up of four judges. When a case is decided in a lower court but there is disagreement about the decision, the court of appeals reviews the case to see if it was handled fairly and without error. Decisions by the court of appeals can be further appealed to the state Supreme Court. Idaho's lower-level courts, where most cases are initially argued, include district courts and trial courts.

How a Bill Becomes a Law

Although new laws can come directly from voters through the initiative process, most state laws come from the legislature. A proposed law, called a bill, goes through many steps in the legislature. Usually, a bill is proposed and introduced in either the state senate or the state house of representatives. Each bill has one or more official sponsor. Once the bill is introduced, the original bill and fifteen copies are given to the secretary of the senate or the chief clerk of the house. He or she assigns it a number. The bill is then read to the senators or representatives, who refer (send) it to a committee for consideration. Committee members examine the bill closely, and often do research, which sometimes leads to asking for changes to parts of the bill. Committees may also hold hearings to receive opinions from experts and interested citizens and get reports from the parties directly affected by the bill. Finally, the committees will decide

Members of the state legislature gather to learn about a proposed bill.

whether to reject the bill or allow it to proceed. Many bills never pass the committee stage.

If the committee supports the bill, it is read a second and third time in the senate or house, where all the members of the chamber can debate, make changes to, and vote on it. If the bill is passed by a majority vote of the members of the chamber where it was introduced, it is sent to the other chamber. There, it goes through the same process as in the first chamber. If the second chamber votes to pass the bill without changing it, it goes

to the governor. But if the second chamber makes changes in the bill before passing it, the full membership of the other chamber must vote on the amended bill.

Once both chambers have passed the bill in the same form, it is sent to the governor to be signed. If the governor signs it, the bill will become law. However, if the governor disapproves of the bill, he or she can veto (reject) it and send it back to the legislature. Often, a bill that is vetoed does not become law. However, if two-thirds of the members of each chamber vote to pass the bill, it will become law despite the governor's disapproval. A measure that the governor has signed or one that the legislature has passed despite his or her veto is then sent to the secretary of state, who assigns it an official number. It is now "on the books" as a state law.

POLITICAL FIGURES
FROM IDAHO

Larry Echo Hawk: Attorney General, 1991-1995

In 1990, Larry Echo Hawk was the first Native American in US history to be elected a state's attorney general. After serving as Idaho's attorney general, he served in the Idaho legislature. From 2009 to 2012, he oversaw Native American matters as an assistant secretary for the US Department of the Interior.

Frank Church: US Senator, 1957-1981

Boise native Frank Church was elected to the US Senate as a young man. An avid environmentalist, he sponsored bills to enact the National Wilderness Act and the Wild and Scenic Rivers Act. He helped establish wilderness areas, including the River of No Return Wilderness that now also bears his name.

Cecil Andrus: Governor, 1971-1977 and 1987-1995

Cecil Andrus served fourteen years over two terms as governor, the longest of anyone in Idaho history. He served as United States Secretary of the Interior for four years when Jimmy Carter was president. He was noted for his environmentalist views, and opposed efforts of the federal government to store nuclear waste in Idaho.

IDAHO
YOU CAN MAKE A DIFFERENCE

★ Contacting Lawmakers

If you are interested in learning more about Idaho's legislators, you can go to **www.legislature.idaho.gov** and click on "Who's My Legislator?" in the left navigation menu. From there, you have several options for identifying your state legislators. You can also go to **www.legislature.idaho.gov/howtocontactlegislators.htm** to find information about how to contact your state legislators by mail, email, or phone.

To contact your national representatives, go to

www.congress.gov

Scroll down to "show current members from" and use the drop-down menu to find Idaho. There are links to each senator and representative there.

★ Students Come First?

In 2011, Idaho's superintendent of public instruction introduced three laws to reform and improve the state's schools. The program was called Students Come First. Three major components in the laws were merit pay for teachers, online classrooms, and a laptop purchased and given to every student. Other parts of the law reduced teachers' retirement pay and moved more control over schools and school budgets to communities, rather than relying on state management. After the law passed, the teachers' union went to court to try and strike down the laws. However, the courts upheld them.

All citizens wanted school reform, but what many parents and teachers saw was that the laws reduced overall funding for schools, and with it teachers' pay and job security. More than one thousand Idaho teachers left the profession in the year after the law was passed. An hour after the laws went into effect, a group called Idaho Parents and Teachers Together filed paperwork with the Idaho secretary of state's office to begin a referendum process that would repeal the laws. The groups sent out thousands of emails, held public meetings, and canvassed in parking lots, street corners, and other public areas collecting signatures to put a referendum on the ballot. They collected seventy-five thousand signatures, enough to put a referendum on the ballot asking voters to repeal the law. On November 6, 2012, the three laws were voted down.

Micron Technology, a major maker of semiconductors, is part of the tech boom based in Boise.

Making a Living

Idaho's wealth of natural beauty is matched only by its wealth of natural resources. Rich mineral deposits are found throughout the state. Fertile soil nourishes a range of crops, including barley, peas, and potatoes. Cattle and sheep graze the plains on farms and ranches, large and small. Thick forests provide construction materials for homes and other buildings. An abundance of water feeds crops, nurtures fish, and provides electricity through use of hydroelectric dams. These are the resources that have helped make Idaho strong. Today, natural resources make up a smaller part of the state's economy than they once did. In their place, other industries have gained a foothold in the state. The people of Idaho have had to embrace change as they assume new jobs and careers.

Agriculture

Soil is one of Idaho's most valuable resources. Several different types of rich and fertile soil are found in the state. In the north, after ancient glaciers retreated during the last Ice Age, they left behind a mixture of various substances that helped make the soil rich. This soil helped give rise to the sprawling forests found in the region. Along the Snake River Plain and in other prairie-like pockets of the state, the soils were formed by tiny pieces of hardened lava and by a material called loess. Many of Idaho's mountain valleys are covered

J.R. Simplot made a pile of money selling French fries made of Idaho potatoes to McDonald's.

in mineral-rich soil, which is made up of substances carried by the state's rivers and streams. This great variety of soils means that many kinds of crops can thrive in different areas across the state.

About twenty-five thousand farms and ranches cover approximately one-fourth of the state. Average farm size is about 450 acres (150 ha). Agriculture is mainly centered on the Snake River Plain. Farmers pump water from the river to make Idaho one of the most irrigated states in the nation. Potatoes are by far the leading crop. Idaho is the top potato-producing state in the United States, accounting for one-third of the nation's potatoes. Hay, alfalfa, and wheat contribute to the state's wealth. Idaho is also a top producer of sugar beets, barley, peas, plums, and mint. The state is one of the world's leading producers of seeds, such as alfalfa, beans, carrot, onion, turnip, and lettuce. Idaho grows 70 percent of all the sweet corn seed produced in the world.

The central and southern plains of Idaho are home to the state's beef and cattle industry. Sheep are also raised. Dairy farms dot the Snake River Valley. Milk and other dairy products, as well as wool, are important sources of agricultural income. Benefitting from cold, clear lakes and rivers, Idaho's farm-raised trout are a valuable food product. Idaho produces more than 70 percent of all trout grown commercially for food in the country.

Mining and Timber

Fifteen million years ago, water heated by volcanoes carried minerals up from rock and deposited them in large clumps throughout Idaho. Today, there are more than eight thousand active and potential mines in the state. Idaho's mines are record holders, especially those in the Silver Valley region of northern Idaho. This area, around Coeur d'Alene, has one of the world's largest concentrations of silver. The Morning Star is one of the deepest mines in the United States, while Bunker Hill ranks as the nation's largest underground mine. The Coeur d'Alene area has survived workers' strikes, blizzards, snow slides, and political disagreements to become one of the richest silver-mining districts in the world. Since the 1880s, the district has produced more than 1.1 billion ounces (31,185 metric tonnes) of silver.

Although a major product, silver is just part of the state's mineral wealth. There is gold in central and southern Idaho; lead, zinc, copper, and antimony in the north; and molybdenum in central Idaho. Other minerals produced include garnets, jasper, jade, limestone, tungsten, clay, and cobalt. Although the north is an especially rich area, valuable mineral deposits are found throughout the state. Phosphate rock, which is used to make fertilizer, comes from Idaho's southeastern corner.

Above ground, the state is graced with valuable resources as well. Forests cover about two-fifths of the state. Idaho is known for its cone-bearing evergreen trees. These include

Phosphate is mined to make fertilizer.

1. Cattle

In 2012, there were 2.2 million head of cattle and calves (including 574,000 dairy cows) in Idaho. July is "Idaho Beef Month," an event celebrating the state's beef industry and promoting knowledge of beef's nutritional value and economic contributions to Idaho.

2. Computer Chips

High-technology industries are relative newcomers to Idaho, but they have provided a new source of jobs. Micron Technology, a leading manufacturer of computer memory chips and other computer components, is based in Boise.

3. Food Processing

The potato, the king of processed foods in Idaho, is sharing the stage with other food products. Litehouse Foods makes salad dressings in Sandpoint. Trout is packaged and sold around the country. So are Chobani yogurt and Clif Bar organic energy bars.

4. Gold

In 2014, gold mining surpassed silver production in Idaho. According to the US Bureau of Mines, Idaho has more mineable gold than any other state. Mining of other minerals is increasing. In 2013, more than $1.1 billion was made by Idaho mines.

5. Potatoes

Idaho produces more than 30 percent of the nation's potatoes. They generate more than $4 billion in revenue each year.

Cattle

Computer Chips

6. Sand and Gravel

Idaho produces more than $500 million each year in sand and gravel. This is a rapidly growing business with so many of the nation's roads and highways needing sand and gravel for required repairs.

7. Seeds

Idaho's Treasure Valley, with plentiful water and sunshine, produces and sells a variety of seeds, including sweet corn, peas, beans, wheat, and clover. Heirloom seeds, from plants that were never genetically altered, are considered healthier and more flavorful.

8. Services

Service industries make up the largest portion of Idaho's economy. Dealers in wholesale goods, such as groceries and wood products lead the industry, along with retailers such as automobile dealerships, grocery stores (Idaho-based Albertson's is a major chain in the Northwest), and restaurants.

9. Tourism

Those who love to ski, fish, cycle, hike, swim, boat, camp, or simply marvel at the beautiful landscape rarely fail to find something to delight them in Idaho. The state has seven national parks, national monuments, and national historic sites, and eleven national natural landmarks.

10. Wood and Paper Products

In 2013, more than $2.4 billion was made from the sale of Idaho's major wood and paper products. Nearly twenty thousand people have timber industry-related jobs.

Tourism

Wood and Paper Products

Recipe for Mashed Potato Pie

Surprise the family at dinner with this delicious side dish, compliments of Idaho's "Famous Potatoes!"

What You Need

3 large russet potatoes

8 ounces (227 g) mozzarella

2 eggs

¾ cup (177.4 milliliters) Parmesan cheese

1/2 cup (118 mL) milk

6 tbsp. (88.7 mL) butter

1/2 cup (118 mL) breadcrumbs

Large soup pot

Mixer (electric is best)

Large mixing spoon

Small mixing bowl

Measuring cups and spoons

Small knife

Fork

Vegetable peeler

Cheese grater

Colander

9-inch by 11-inch (23 by 28 cm) or
         9-inch circular roasting pan

What To Do

- Preheat oven 350 degrees Fahrenheit (176°C)
- Bring 3 cups of water (0.71 L) to boil. Peel and quarter potatoes; boil potatoes 20 minutes or until soft.
- Meanwhile, cut butter and mozzarella into small pieces. Grate Parmesan cheese. Lightly stir eggs with fork, set all items aside.
- Drain cooked potatoes and return them to pot. Add 4 tbsp. butter pieces and mash with spoon. Then beat with electric mixer until creamy. Mix in (using spoon) mozzarella, milk, and eggs. Add Parmesan, mix again.
- Using butter wrapper, grease bottom and sides of pan and scatter bottom with ¼ cup (59 mL) breadcrumbs. Spread mashed potato mixture into pan. On top of mixture, scatter remaining butter pieces and breadcrumbs.
- Bake, uncovered 40 minutes, until golden.
- Serve with pride!

High-Tech Ground

In 2013, miners discovered a large underground vein of "**rare earth**" minerals at Lemhi Pass. Rare earth minerals are used in making parts for cell phones, computers, televisions, video consoles, and other electronic devices. They are also used to make batteries that store power for windmills and hybrid cars.

Douglas fir, Engelmann spruce, hemlock, lodgepole pine, red cedar, western larch, white fir, and white pine. But deciduous trees, which lose their leaves in winter, blanket parts of the state as well. Birch, cottonwood, and aspen line rivers and cover the hillsides.

Idaho is the eighth-largest lumber-producing state in the United States. Forest products companies operate in many Idaho counties. The state's forest products industry produces nearly $2 billion worth of wood and paper products each year. Boise Cascade, a major manufacturer of wood products and building materials, has its headquarters in Boise.

Manufacturing

In recent years, manufacturing has grown to become an important part of Idaho's economy. Food processing is a major Idaho industry, especially potato processing. There are also dairies, meatpacking plants, and businesses that process sugar beets and wheat. New companies producing food products for the nation reflect Idaho's outdoorsy, healthy character.

The electronics industry has proved to be big business for the Gem State. Computer and electronic products now make up the state's largest category of manufactured goods. Idaho factories also create metal and wood products, machinery, plastic and rubber products, chemicals, and medical devices.

All this activity accounts for 11 percent of the gross state product, the total amount of goods and services produced in the state each year. Some $6.2 billion worth of products were made in Idaho in 2013. They were shipped across the state, throughout the country, and around the world.

Services

While manufacturing is important to Idaho, the state's many service industries are even more so. Teachers, librarians, restaurant and retail workers, real estate agents, bankers, lawyers, insurance agents, health care workers, firefighters, and police officers are some

A factory in Caldwell manufactures tortillas.

of the service industry positions Idahoans fill. Most service jobs are found in and around the state's cities and large towns, but certainly not all. Forest rangers, rural shopkeepers, livestock veterinarians, and vendors of farm equipment and supplies all pursue their trades often far from the beaten path.

Tourism is an important source of income for the state. The tourist industry brings in nearly $3 billion a year and provides jobs for twenty-six thousand people. More than twenty million people visit Idaho each year. Some come to hike in the wilderness, ski at Sun Valley or Schweitzer Mountain, or ride the rapids on the Salmon River. Others come to trace the steps of pioneers and miners from long ago. Still others come to marvel at the state's many beautiful sights, including the Clearwater National Forest, Bruneau Dunes State Park, Craters of the Moon National Monument, Hells Canyon, and Shoshone Falls.

The Two Faces of Idaho

In many ways today, Idaho is divided in two: One part is urban (people living in and around cities), and one part is more rural. One of the major shifts the state has faced in the past one hundred years or so is where its residents choose to live. In 1900, 6 percent of Idaho's population lived in cities. By 2010, that proportion had climbed to more than 65 percent. Census figures indicated that between 2000 and 2010, 80 percent of Idaho's population growth

White-water rafting is one of the many outdoor adventures attracting tourists to Idaho.

came in its eleven metropolitan counties. As a result, some small towns are shrinking. They offer little to lure young people, who often have to look elsewhere to find jobs that pay well.

The state's "Old West" economy, based on timber, mining, and agriculture, is losing ground. Stiff competition from other states and nations, lower prices for some commodities, and the rapid shift in technology are just a few of the reasons. While one way of life is slowly fading, another has emerged to replace it. The "New West" economy has turned to high-tech industries and tourism to create jobs.

The gap between rich and poor in Idaho, often the difference between urban and rural lifestyles, has grown wider. On average, Idaho residents living in urban areas earn more than those who live in rural areas. Rural communities are now looking for new directions and exploring new paths. The state government established the Idaho Rural Partnership, drawing upon both public and private resources, to strengthen rural Idaho communities and improve their quality of life. Idaho citizens have always shown a remarkable sense of independence and self-reliance. The Idaho Rural Partnership wants rural communities to grow and change in the way they want. Likewise, Idaho's urban communities are set with the task of managing a growing economy, while keeping the state's natural resources healthy for future generations. It will be a shared responsibility for all of Idaho's citizens to preserve their history and culture while moving forward.

IDAHO
STATE MAP

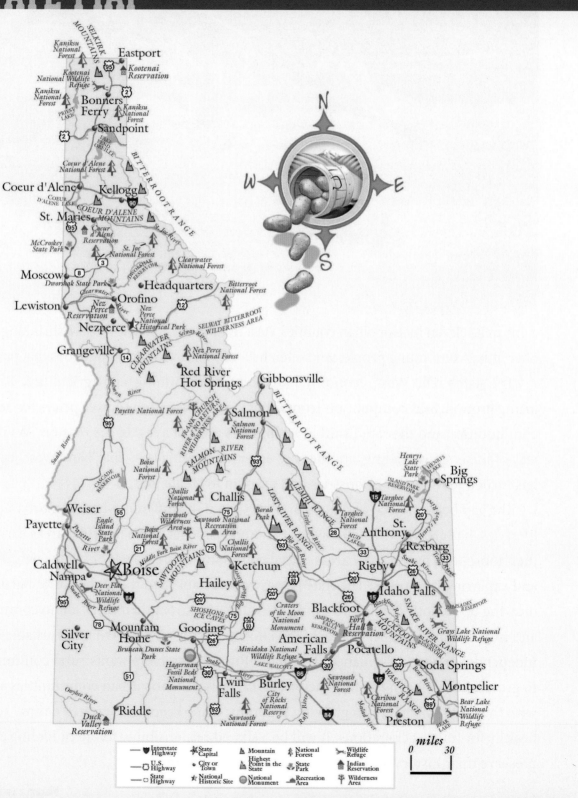

Kaniksu National Forest
Eastport
SELKIRK MOUNTAINS
Kootenai National Wildlife Refuge
Kootenai Reservation
Kaniksu National Forest
Bonners Ferry
Kaniksu National Forest
PRIEST LAKE
Sandpoint
LAKE PEND OREILLE
Coeur d'Alene National Forest
BITTERROOT RANGE
Coeur d'Alene
COEUR D'ALENE LAKE
Kellogg
COEUR D'ALENE MOUNTAINS
St. Maries
Coeur d'Alene Reservation
McCroskey State Park
St. Joe National Forest
St. Joe River
DWORSHAK RESERVOIR
Clearwater National Forest
Moscow
Dworshak State Park
Clearwater River
Headquarters
Bitterroot National Forest
Orofino
Nez Perce Reservation
Nez Perce National Historical Park
Lewiston
Clearwater River
Nezperce
SELWAY BITTERROOT WILDERNESS AREA
Selway River
Grangeville
CLEARWATER MOUNTAINS
Nez Perce National Forest
Salmon River
Red River Hot Springs
Gibbonsville
BITTERROOT RANGE
Payette National Forest
FRANK CHURCH RIVER OF NO RETURN WILDERNESS AREA
Salmon
Salmon National Forest
Snake River
Boise National Forest
SALMON RIVER MOUNTAINS
LEMHI RANGE
Henrys Lake State Park
HENRYS LAKE
Big Springs
CASCADE RESERVOIR
Challis National Forest
Challis
LOST RIVER RANGE
Little Lost River
ISLAND PARK RESERVOIR
Targhee National Forest
Weiser
Sawtooth Wilderness Area
Sawtooth National Recreation Area
Borah Peak
Targhee National Forest
St. Anthony
Payette
Eagle Island State Park
Boise National Forest
Challis National Forest
Big Lost River
28
MUD LAKE
33
Rexburg
Payette River
Middle Fork Boise River
Snake River
33
Caldwell
Boise
SAWTOOTH MOUNTAINS
Ketchum
Rigby
Snake River
Nampa
Hailey
20
Idaho Falls
Deer Flat National Wildlife Refuge
Snake River
Big Wood River
Craters of the Moon National Monument
Blackfoot
SNAKE RIVER RANGE
PALISADES RESERVOIR
Mountain Home
SHOSHONE ICE CAVES
Gooding
AMERICAN FALLS RESERVOIR
Fort Hall Reservation
BLACKFOOT MOUNTAINS
Blackfoot River
Grays Lake National Wildlife Refuge
Silver City
Bruneau Dunes State Park
American Falls
Minidoka National Wildlife Refuge
Pocatello
Snake River
Hagerman Fossil Beds National Monument
LAKE WALCOTT
Soda Springs
WASATCH RANGE
Owyhee River
Twin Falls
Burley
Sawtooth National Forest
Montpelier
Bear River
Riddle
City of Rocks National Reserve
Caribou National Forest
Bear Lake National Wildlife Refuge
Duck Valley Reservation
Sawtooth National Forest
Preston
BEAR LAKE
Raft River
Malad River

Legend:
- Interstate Highway
- U.S. Highway
- State Highway
- State Capital
- City or Town
- National Historic Site
- Mountain
- Highest Point in the State
- National Monument
- National Forest
- State Park
- Recreation Area
- Wildlife Refuge
- Indian Reservation
- Wilderness Area

miles
0   30

IDAHO
MAP SKILLS

1. **What city lies closest to the Kootenai Reservation?**

2. **What is the name of the wildlife refuge in the southeast corner of the state?**

3. **Which city is nearest Pocatello, Twin Falls or American Falls?**

4. **Which of these cities is not on Interstate 84, Gooding, Boise, or Orofino?**

5. **Is Salmon National Forest east or west of Payette National Forest?**

6. **If you were driving from Soda Springs to Lewiston, which direction would you be going?**

7. **Which pair of cities are closer to each other? Nampa and Caldwell or Moscow and Kellogg?**

8. **Which of these mountain ranges does not share a border with another state or country? Bitterroot, Selkirk, or Clearwater?**

9. **Which city is farther from Lake Coeur d'Alene, Sandpoint or Bonner's Ferry?**

10. **Which site is closest to Boise, Nez Perce National Historical Park or Craters of the Moon National Monument?**

Bear Lake

10. Craters of the Moon National Monument
9. Bonner's Ferry
8. Clearwater
7. Nampa and Caldwell
6. Northwest
5. East
4. Orofino
3. American Falls
2. Bear Lake National Wildlife Refuge
1. Eastport

State Flag, Seal, and Song

The Idaho flag is dark blue with the state seal in the middle. A red scroll reading "State of Idaho" is beneath the seal. The flag was adopted by the state legislature in 1907. Since there were different versions of the state seal, the flag was readopted with the new seal in 1957. The original flag that flew atop the state capitol building in 1907 is on display at the Idaho Historical Museum.

The state seal was created in 1890 and adopted in 1891 as the first act of the Idaho legislature. It shows a woman at the left holding the scales of justice. She stands for equality. The miner at the right represents mining's importance to the state. The elk's head in the center stands for Idaho's wildlife, the pine tree for its forests, and the grain and fruits on the bottom for the state's farming industry. The seal was designed by Emma Edwards Green. She is the only woman to design a state seal in the United States. In 1957, the seal was updated and streamlined by Paul B. Evans.

The state song is "Here We Have Idaho," with words by Albert Tompkins and McKinley Helm and music by Sallie Hume-Douglas. The music was copyrighted on November 4, 1915, under the title "Garden of Paradise." The words were added later. It was adopted as the state song by the Idaho legislature on March 11, 1931.

Lyrics can be found on Idaho's official website: **gov.idaho.gov/about/song.html**

Glossary

camas	An edible wild bulb in the lily family found in the western United States.
conservation	The careful use of natural resources to prevent them from being lost or wasted.
deciduous	A tree marked by shedding or losing foliage at the end of the growing season.
fossil	A preserved remnant of a plant or animal from an older geologic age.
geyser	A natural hot spring that ejects a column of water and steam into the air.
Great Depression	The worldwide economic collapse beginning in 1929 and continuing until the late 1930s.
initiative	In government, a procedure where citizens can propose a law and vote to have it approved.
invasive species	Non-native plant or animal that spreads and takes over native species.
irrigation	A system of pumps, pipes and/or canals that draws fresh water from lakes and rivers and delivers it to crop fields.
lava	Hot, melted rock that issues from a volcano or crack in the earth.
missionary	A person who goes to a place far from home to spread religious beliefs and/or to help people who are poor or sick.
nomads	People who move from place to place.
rare earth	A mixture of metals and minerals found deep in the earth that is widely distributed but usually only found in small deposits.
referendum	In government, a procedure where citizens can propose to repeal a law and vote to have the repeal approved.
reservation [Native American]	An area of land in the US that is kept separate as a place for Native Americans to live.

More About Idaho

BOOKS

Biskup, Agnieszka. *Thunder Rolling Down the Mountains*. Mankato, MN: Capstone Press, 2011.

Ditchfield, Christin. *The Shoshone*. New York: Franklin Watts, 2005.

Gish, Melissa. *Bison*. Mankato, MN: Creative Education, 2012.

Lusted, Marcia Amidon. *Idaho: The Gem State*. New York: Powerkids Press, 2010.

Norwich, Grace. *I Am: Sacagawea*. New York: Scholastic, 2012.

Stanley, John. *Idaho Past and Present*. New York: Rosen Publishing, 2010.

WEBSITES

Idaho Animals

idahoptv.org/dialogue4kids/archive/animals.cfm

Idaho's Official State Website

www.state.id.us

ABOUT THE AUTHORS

Doug Sanders is a writer and editor who lives in New York. He has written five other titles in the It's My State! series.

Jacqueline Laks Gorman has been a writer and editor for more than thirty years. She and her family live in DeKalb, Illinois.

Ruth Bjorklund lives on an island near Seattle, Washington. She has the very good fortune to live near, and be able to explore, the beautiful state of Idaho.

Index

Index